ON THE COVER

Ice forming on Sprague Lake early in November at Rocky Mountain National Park, Colorado.
Credit: National Park Service.

ON THIS PAGE

Alluvial fan, just west of Horseshoe Park at Rocky Mountain National Park, Colorado.
Credit: National Park Service.

2010 Monitoring and Tracking Wet Nitrogen Deposition at Rocky Mountain National Park

August 2012

Natural Resource Report NPS/NRSS/ARD/NRR—2012/562

Kristi Morris
National Park Service, Air Resources Division

Alisa Mast
Dave Clow
U.S. Geological Survey, Rocky Mountain Region, Colorado Water Science Center

Greg Wetherbee
U.S. Geological Survey, Branch of Quality Systems, NADP External QA Project

Jill Baron
U.S. Geological Survey, Colorado State University—Natural Resource Ecology Laboratory

Curt Taipale
Colorado Department of Public Health and Environment, Air Pollution Control Division

Tamara Blett
National Park Service, Air Resources Division

David Gay
NADP Program Officer, Program Coordinator

Eric Richer
National Ecological Observatory Network

August 2012

U.S. Department of the Interior
National Park Service
Natural Resource Stewardship and Science
Denver, Colorado

The National Park Service, Natural Resource Stewardship and Science office in Denver, Colorado publishes a range of reports that address natural resource topics of interest and applicability to a broad audience in the National Park Service and others in natural resource management, including scientists, conservation and environmental constituencies, and the public.

The Natural Resource Report Series is used to disseminate high-priority, current natural resource management information with managerial application. The series targets a general, diverse audience, and may contain NPS policy considerations or address sensitive issues of management applicability.

All manuscripts in the series receive the appropriate level of peer review to ensure that the information is scientifically credible, technically accurate, appropriately written for the intended audience, and designed and published in a professional manner. This report received formal, high-level peer review based on the importance of its content, or its potentially controversial or precedent-setting nature. Peer review was conducted by highly qualified individuals with subject area technical expertise and was overseen by a peer review manager.

Views, statements, findings, conclusions, recommendations, and data in this report do not necessarily reflect views and policies of the National Park Service, U.S. Department of the Interior. Mention of trade names or commercial products does not constitute endorsement or recommendation for use by the U.S. Government.

This report is available from the Air Resources Division of the NPS (www.nature.nps/air/pubs/pdf/rmnp-trends/rmnp-trends_2010.pdf) and the Natural Resource Publications Management Web site (http://www.nature.nps.gov/publications/nrpm) on the Internet.

Please cite this publication as:

Morris, K., A. Mast, D. Clow, G. Wetherbee, J. Baron, C. Taipale, T. Blett, D. Gay, and E. Richer. 2012. 2010 monitoring and tracking wet nitrogen deposition at Rocky Mountain National Park: August 2012. Natural Resource Report NPS/NRSS/ARD/NRR—2012/562. National Park Service, Denver, Colorado.

NPS 121/116432, August 2012

Contents

Tables

Figures

Acknowledgements

The authors acknowledge Chris Lehmann, Mark Rhodes, Jim Cheatham, and Lisa Clarke for their participation in numerous scientific discussions regarding the tracking of nitrogen deposition data. The authors also thank John Vimont, Susan Johnson, Doug Druliner, Kathy Tonnessen, and Mark Nilles for their careful review of the report. Finally, the authors would like to thank all of the volunteers that have helped maintain and operate the monitoring sites referenced in this report. Any use of trade, product, or firm names is for descriptive purposes only and does not imply endorsement by the U.S. Government.

1. Background Information on the Nitrogen Deposition Reduction Plan

In 2004, a multi-agency meeting including the Colorado Department of Public Health and Environment (CDPHE), the National Park Service (NPS), and the U.S. Environmental Protection Agency (EPA) was held to address the effects and trends of nitrogen deposition and related air quality issues at Rocky Mountain National Park (RMNP). These agencies signed a Memorandum of Understanding (MOU) to facilitate interagency coordination, calling the effort the "Rocky Mountain National Park Initiative." After much collaboration, the MOU agencies (CDPHE, NPS, and EPA) issued the Nitrogen Deposition Reduction Plan (NDRP) in 2007, which was endorsed by the three agencies and the Colorado Air Quality Control Commission (AQCC). The NDRP and other related documents are available on the CDPHE website, http://www.cdphe.state.co.us/ap/rmnp.html.

As part of the NDRP, the NPS adopted and the MOU agencies endorsed a wet deposition level of 1.5 kilograms of nitrogen per hectare per year (kg N/ha/yr) as an appropriate science-based threshold for identifying adverse ecosystem effects in RMNP. This threshold is based on decades of research and is the "critical load" of nitrogen that can be absorbed by sensitive ecosystems within RMNP before detrimental changes occur (Baron et al. 2006). To achieve this threshold, referred to as the resource management goal, the MOU agencies have chosen a glidepath approach. This type of approach anticipates gradual improvement over time and is a commonly used regulatory structure for long-term, goal-oriented air quality planning.

The glidepath approach allows for the resource management goal for RMNP to be met over the course of 25 years. The baseline wet deposition condition at Loch Vale in RMNP is 3.1 kg N/ha/yr based on data from 2002–2006. The first interim milestone is based on a reduction of wet nitrogen deposition from baseline conditions to 2.7 kg N/ha/yr by the year 2012. Progress towards this and subsequent interim milestones will be assessed using the weight of evidence at 5 year intervals starting in 2013 until the resource management goal is achieved in the year 2032. The weight of evidence approach relies on a variety of relevant information in the decision making process. Further explanation is provided in Section 5 of this report.

The NDRP required that a Contingency Plan be developed to put in place corrective measures in the event that the initial 2012 milestone and any subsequent interim

Subalpine meadow ecosystems are sensitive to the effects of nutrient enrichment from atmospheric deposition.
Credit: National Park Service.

milestones are not achieved. The Nitrogen Deposition Data Tracking Plan was included as Appendix B of the Contingency Plan (http://www.cdphe.state.co.us/ap/rmnp/RMNPContingencyPlanFinal.pdf). To continuously track nitrogen deposition at the park, the MOU agencies will annually update the data analysis with the most recent year's data. This analysis will be published annually in a peer-reviewed NPS report.

The MOU agencies will meet by September of each year to discuss the analyses and determine whether the Contingency Plan should be revised based on new information. In the years following the interim milestones (and within 180 days of the issuance of the deposition data), the MOU agencies will evaluate how nitrogen deposition is changing at RMNP and determine whether an interim milestone was achieved. If the agencies concur that a milestone was not achieved, the contingency process will be triggered.

2. Purpose

The purpose of this report is to inform the MOU agencies, stakeholders, and the public about the current status and trends of wet nitrogen deposition at RMNP. The MOU agencies will use the information provided in this annual report to make a determination of whether the interim milestones have been achieved in 2013, 2018, 2023, and 2028.

3. Monitoring Wet Nitrogen Deposition

The resource management goal and interim milestones identified in the NDRP are based on wet nitrogen (N)[1] deposition data at Loch Vale in RMNP that are collected through the National Atmospheric Deposition Program/National Trends Network (NADP/NTN). The NADP/NTN is a nationwide precipitation chemistry monitoring network and a cooperative effort between many different groups, including the U.S. Geological Survey, EPA, NPS, U.S. Department of Agriculture, State Agricultural Experiment Stations, U.S. Fish and Wildlife Service, and numerous universities and other governmental and private entities. The NADP/NTN began monitoring in 1978 with 22 sites but grew rapidly in the early 1980s. Much of the expansion occurred during the implementation of monitoring under the National Acid Precipitation Assessment Program. Today the network has over 250 sites spanning the continental U.S., Alaska, Puerto Rico, and the Virgin Islands.

The purpose of the network is to collect data and monitor geographical patterns for long-term trends in precipitation chemistry. The precipitation at each site is collected weekly according to strict clean-handling procedures. The sample is then sent to the NADP Central Analytical Laboratory in Champaign, Ill., where it is analyzed for pH, specific conductance, and sulfate, nitrate, ammonium, chloride, calcium, magnesium, potassium, and sodium concentrations. Stringent quality assurance and quality control programs ensure that the data are accurate and precise. More information on these programs and the monitoring data can be found on the NADP/NTN website at http://nadp.isws.illinois.edu. Annual data are generally available on the website six months after completion of the calendar year.

NADP/NTN data are used widely in publications, including nearly 150 peer-reviewed journal articles in 2011. Data also are used extensively by the EPA to assess progress made by the Clean Air Act Acid Rain Program, which seeks to reduce U.S. emissions of sulfur dioxide (SO_2) and nitrogen oxides (NO_X). (U.S. EPA 2011 and 2012). NADP data also are the cornerstone of the "National Acid Precipitation Assessment

High elevation streams at Rocky Mountain National Park are sensitive to acidification from nitrogen and sulfur pollution. Credit: National Park Service.

Program Report to Congress 2011" (Burns et al. 2011) and used to assess progress under the U.S.-Canada Air Quality Agreement (U.S. EPA 2010).

4. Monitoring in Rocky Mountain National Park

There are two NADP/NTN sites in RMNP. The Loch Vale site is located at a high elevation of 3,159 m (10,362 ft) and the Beaver Meadows site is located at a lower elevation of 2,490 m (8,169 ft). Both sites have been operating since the early 1980s. Data from the Loch Vale site are the primary focus of the NDRP because the resource management goal of 1.5 kg N/ha/yr wet deposition is based on NADP/NTN data from this site. The resource management goal was set to protect the most sensitive resources in the park which also are at the highest elevations.

Routine monitoring in a remote, high elevation location presents several challenges. The samples from Loch Vale are collected each week by a dedicated site operator who hikes or skis in 5 km (approximately 3 miles) to the monitoring site year-round. Equipment malfunction and/or inadequate solar power supply during the harsh winter months sometimes result in missed samples. Due to the importance of these data in tracking deposition, the MOU agencies agreed to co-locate a second NADP/NTN monitoring site at Loch Vale, which was installed in September of 2009. Since that time, the site has included two precipitation collectors and two electronic rain gages. The original mechanical rain gage was operated for two years for comparison to the electronic gages and then was removed. In 2010, solar panels and batteries were upgraded to increase power supply and storage. Telemetry also was added to the site to

---

[1] The nitrogen measured by NADP/NTN is inorganic, and all references to wet nitrogen deposition in this report refer to the inorganic portion of nitrogen deposition only.

allow equipment and/or power issues to be identified quickly and resolved during the following weekly site visit. In fall 2011, the four solar panels were replaced with two more efficient, less reflective panels and moved to a location of less snow accumulation. Appendix A provides a history of the Loch Vale monitoring site. Also in 2011, two ammonia passive samplers were installed at RMNP as part of the NADP Ammonia Monitoring Network (AMoN). One site was installed at the Loch Vale NADP site and one at the Clean Air Status and Trends Network (CASTNet) site near the Long's Peak Ranger Station at an elevation of 2,743 m (8,999 ft). Data from these two sites are available at http://nadp.isws.illinois.edu/AMoN/ and will be presented in future reports.

5. Tracking Wet Nitrogen Deposition at Rocky Mountain National Park

The interim milestones in the NDRP are based on a 5 year rolling average of the annual wet nitrogen deposition data from the Loch Vale NADP/NTN site in RMNP (http://nadp.sws.uiuc.edu/sites/siteinfo.asp?id=CO98&net= NTN). The first interim milestone of the NDRP calls for this 5 year rolling average of wet nitrogen deposition at the park to be reduced from the baseline loading of 3.1 kg N/ha/yr in 2006 to 2.7 kg N/ha/yr in 2012. Another goal of the NDRP is to "reverse the trend of increasing nitrogen deposition at the park." Determination of the success or failure of the goals of the NDRP will be made using the weight of evidence. Several analyses will be used to track nitrogen deposition at RMNP. These analyses may be modified as additional information becomes available and will include the following: (1) assessment of progress along the glidepath, (2) long-term (>20 years) trend analyses for RMNP and other regional sites, and (3) short-term (5 and 7 years) trend analyses for RMNP and other regional sites. Each section below describes the details of the analyses and shows the results for the analyses ending in 2010.

5.1. Assessment of progress along the glidepath

This assessment compares current wet nitrogen deposition (calculated as the most recent 5 year average) at the original Loch Vale NADP/NTN site to the interim milestones on the NDRP glidepath. Annual wet nitrogen deposition is calculated by multiplying the annual precipitation-weighted mean nitrogen concentration by the annual amount of precipitation (see Appendix B for explanation of NADP/NTN terms and calculations). Therefore, deposition values are influenced by the amount of precipitation in any given year, including wet years and dry years. Using a rolling 5 year average of wet nitrogen deposition reduces the inter-annual variability caused by year to year variation in precipitation. Data were obtained from the NADP/NTN website and screened according to the data completeness criteria described in Appendix C.

Figure 1 shows the glidepath from the NDRP. The first interim milestone is 2.7 kg N/ha/yr of wet deposition in 2012, followed by three more interim milestones at 5 year intervals, eventually resulting in a wet deposition of 1.5 kg N/ha/yr and achievement of the resource management goal in 2032. The estimate for nitrogen deposition under natural pre-industrial conditions, 0.2 kg N/ha/yr also is shown in Figure 1 (Galloway et al. 1995 and 1996; Dentener 2001).

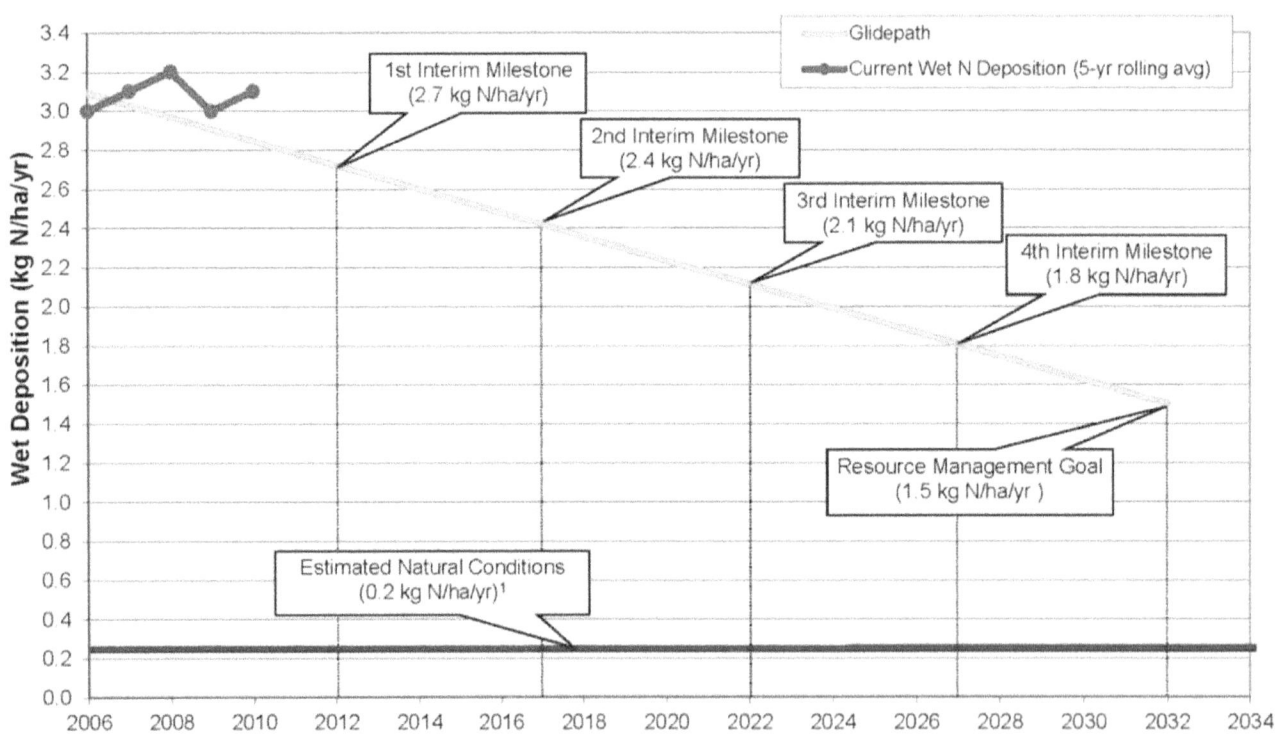

Figure 1. Glidepath and current wet nitrogen deposition at Loch Vale in Rocky Mountain National Park.
[1] Galloway et al. 1995 and 1996; Dentener 2001.

The glidepath model provides the foundation for the weight of evidence approach in assessing milestones, and allows us to answer the question: Is current wet nitrogen deposition in RMNP on or below the glidepath? Current wet nitrogen deposition (5 year rolling average) is shown in Figure 1 for 2006 through 2010. In 2010, the calculated 5 year average (2006–2010) of wet nitrogen deposition was 3.1 kg N/ha/yr. This value represents a 0.25 kg N/ha/yr departure from the glidepath in Figure 1. Therefore, the answer to the question is: no, wet nitrogen deposition was not on or below the glidepath in 2010. NADP/NTN quality assurance programs have estimated uncertainty in the measurements by operating co-located sites (duplicate sets of NADP/NTN instrumentation) annually within the NADP/NTN network since 1986 (Wetherbee et al. 2005). These sites are typically moved year to year to test variability in different geographic areas. Only three of the sites have been located in western high elevation ecosystems. The data collected from the co-located site at Loch Vale (installation in fall 2009) will be used to estimate site-specific uncertainty in the measurements and will provide three full years of data before 2013 when the MOU agencies will determine

whether the first interim milestone has been achieved. The data from the original NADP site at Loch Vale will always be used to compare to the glidepath because the resource management goal is based on hindcasting of data from this site. A comparison of data from the co-located sites for 2010 is shown in Appendix D.

Figure 2 shows the annual and 5 year rolling average of wet nitrogen deposition at the Loch Vale NADP/NTN site from 1984–2010. Annual precipitation and the long-term average precipitation (1984–2010) also are shown. The 5 year rolling average of wet nitrogen deposition increased in the 1990s during a period of above average precipitation and following a period of below average annual precipitation and deposition from 1987–1989. However, it has been relatively stable since then, even as Colorado experienced an extended period of drought starting in 1998. In 2009 and 2010, annual precipitation amount was well above the long-term average. Figure 2 also shows that annual deposition has varied around the first interim milestone (2.7 kg N/ha/yr) during the past decade, including in 2009 when annual deposition was 2.8 kg N/ha/yr during a year with above average precipitation.

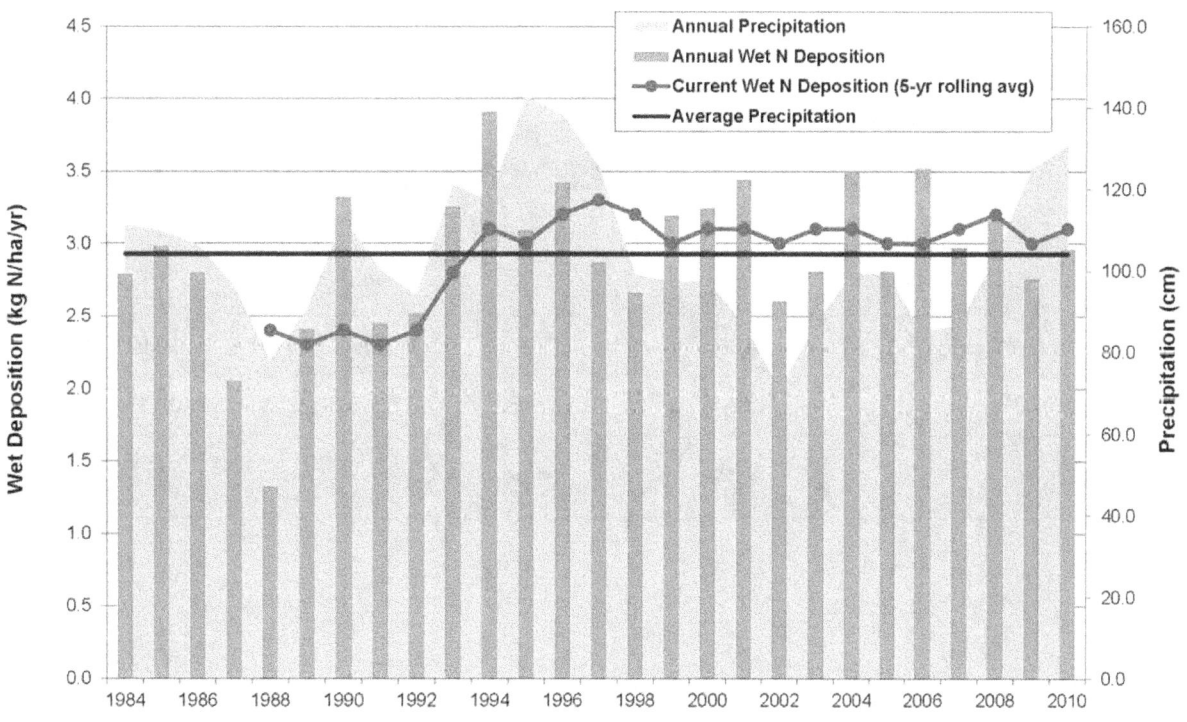

Figure 2. Wet nitrogen deposition and precipitation at Loch Vale in Rocky Mountain National Park.

5.2. Long-term trends analyses for Rocky Mountain National Park and other regional sites

The NPS began monitoring precipitation chemistry at Loch Vale in 1983. Changes in nitrogen in precipitation were evaluated over the 26-year period of record. Statistical trends on several different parameters provide information on how nitrogen has changed over time and whether nitrogen inputs to park ecosystems have increased, decreased, or remained unchanged. The parameters include wet nitrogen (N) deposition (kg N/ha/yr), precipitation-weighted mean nitrate (NO_3^-) and ammonium (NH_4^+) concentrations (μeq/L), and precipitation depth (cm). Each parameter provides different information. Trends analyses on deposition data provide ecological relevance to the resource management goal for RMNP. Trends analyses on concentrations provide information more closely coupled to air quality at individual sites and allow for comparison among sites.

In order to compare data from Loch Vale with other sites exposed to similar Front Range emissions, three NADP/NTN sites located outside of the park and the two original NADP/NTN sites that are located within RMNP are included in the analyses. These additional sites provide regional context and are listed in Table 1 and shown in Figure 3. The NADP/NTN sites at Niwot Saddle (3,520 m) and Sugarloaf (2,524 m) are located in the mountains 26.6 km and 36.2 km southeast of Loch Vale, respectively. The sites complement each other as paired high elevation and low elevation monitoring sites, just like Loch Vale and Beaver Meadows in RMNP. The NADP/NTN site at Pawnee is at a much lower elevation (1,641 m), located 96 km east of Loch Vale in the plains.

Figure 4a–e shows the annual data for the period of record at each of the five sites for deposition, concentration, and precipitation. General patterns are identified below; however, please note that the scales for each graph are different for each site in order to best show patterns over time. Precipitation amount has varied substantially among these five Front Range sites over the periods of record, which range from 24–31 years among the sites. The higher elevation sites record much more precipitation than their lower elevation counterparts. Pawnee (at the lowest elevation) records the least amount of precipitation.

Table 1. NADP/NTN sites in and near Rocky Mountain National Park used in trends analyses.

Site Name	NADP/NTN Site ID	Period of Record	Elevation	Distance to Loch Vale
Loch Vale (RMNP)	CO98	27 yrs	3,159 m (10,364 ft)	–
Beaver Meadows (RMNP)	CO19	31 yrs	2,490 m (8,169 ft)	11 km (6.8 mi)
Niwot Saddle	CO02	27 yrs	3,520 m (11,549 ft)	26.6 km (16.5 mi)
Sugarloaf	CO94	24 yrs	2,524 m (8,281 ft)	36.2 km (22.5 mi)
Pawnee	CO22	31 yrs	1,641 m (5,384 ft)	96 km (59.7 mi)

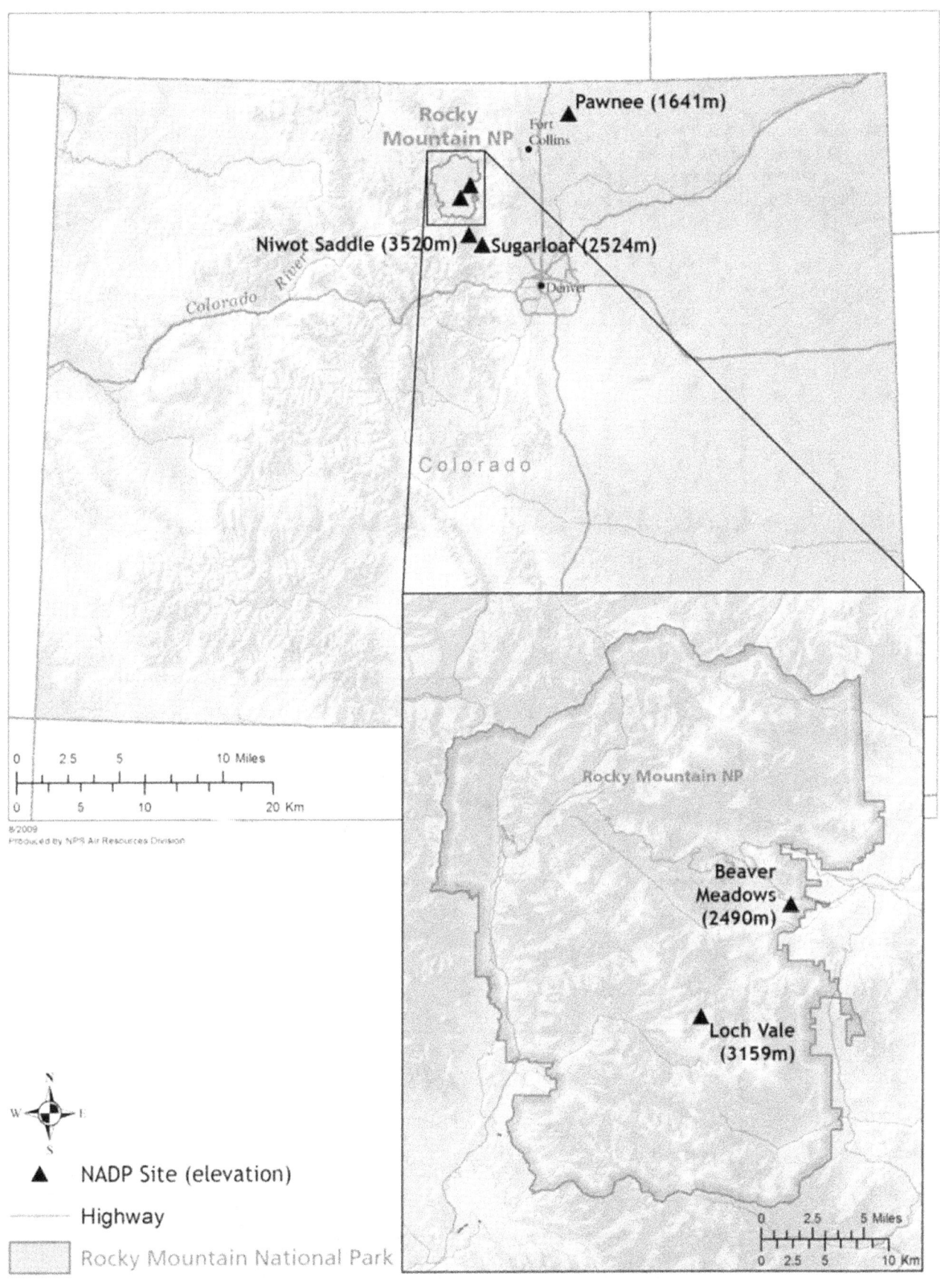

Figure 3. Map of NADP/NTN sites in and near Rocky Mountain National Park.

In general, wet nitrogen deposition ranges from 2–4 kg N/ha/yr at all Front Range sites, except for Niwot Saddle, where deposition is much higher, due to the over collection of snow (Williams et al., 1998). Annual ammonium deposition and nitrate deposition are contributing almost equal parts to nitrogen deposition at Loch Vale, Beaver Meadows, and Sugarloaf. Nitrate deposition is higher than ammonium deposition at Niwot Saddle, and ammonium deposition is higher than nitrate deposition at Pawnee.

Nitrate and ammonium concentrations are generally in the same range among all sites, except for Pawnee, where concentrations are much higher. Nitrate concentrations are slightly higher than ammonium concentrations at all the sites, except for Pawnee where ammonium concentrations are distinctly higher. Concentrations are typically lower at the high elevation sites, where precipitation amount is greater.

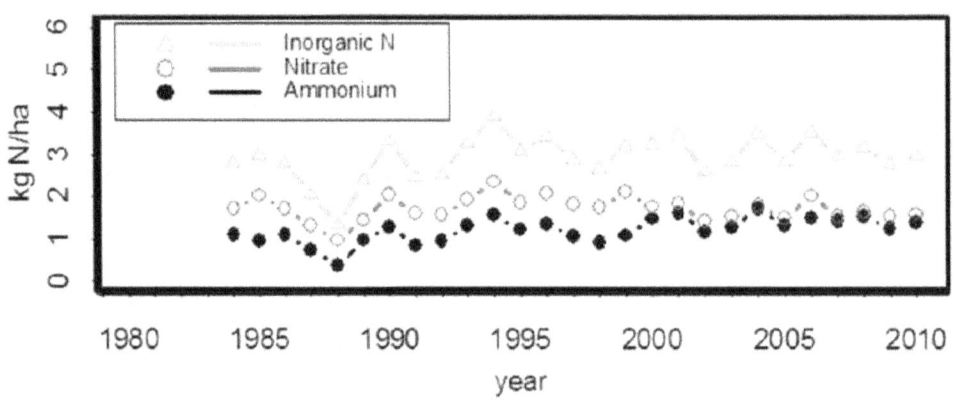

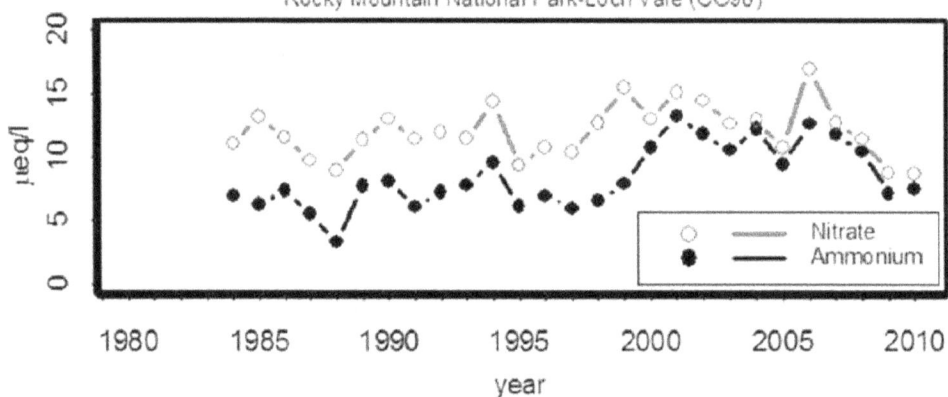

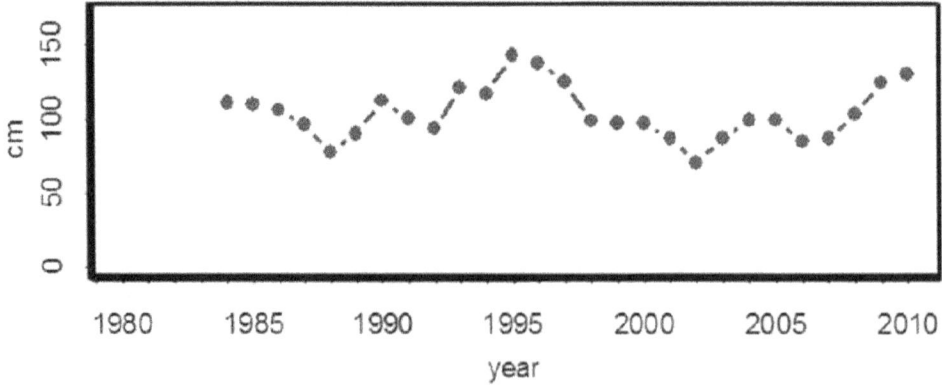

Figure 4a. Deposition, concentrations, and precipitation for Loch Vale.

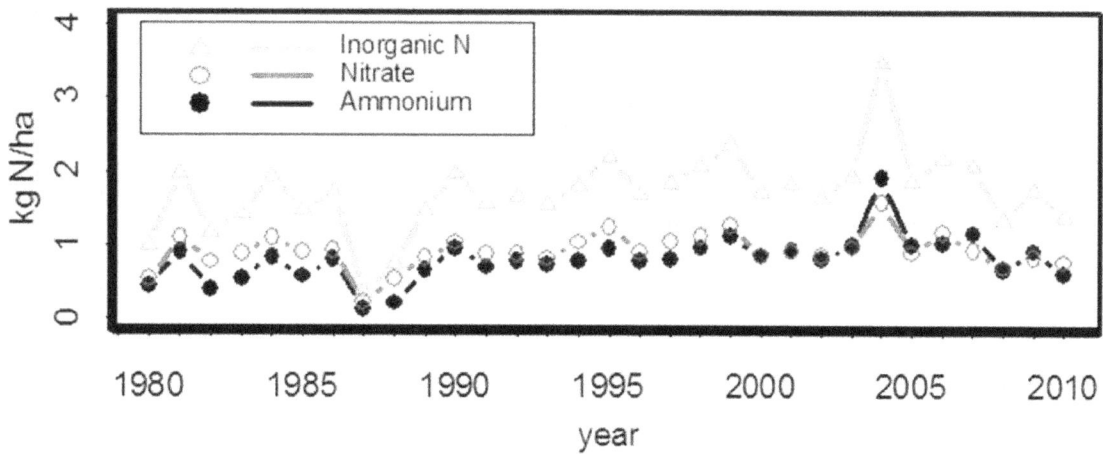

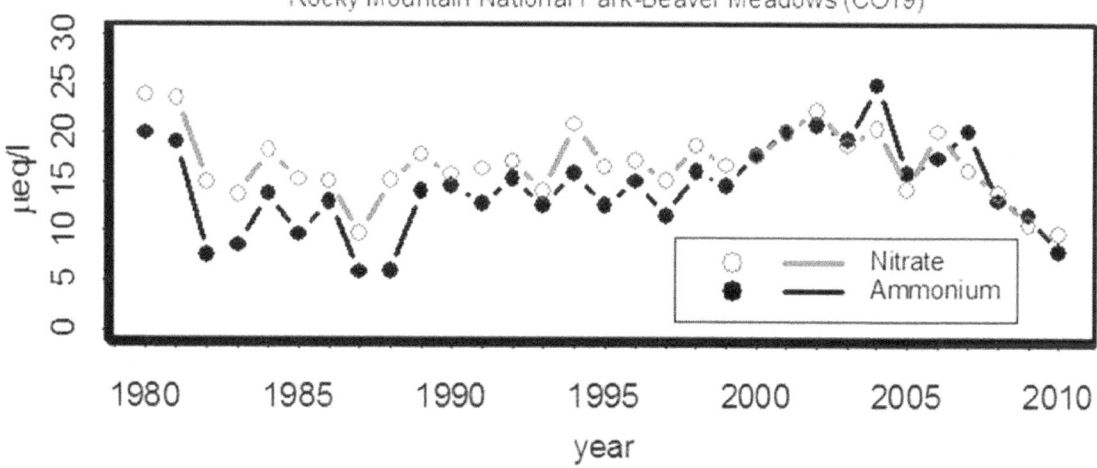

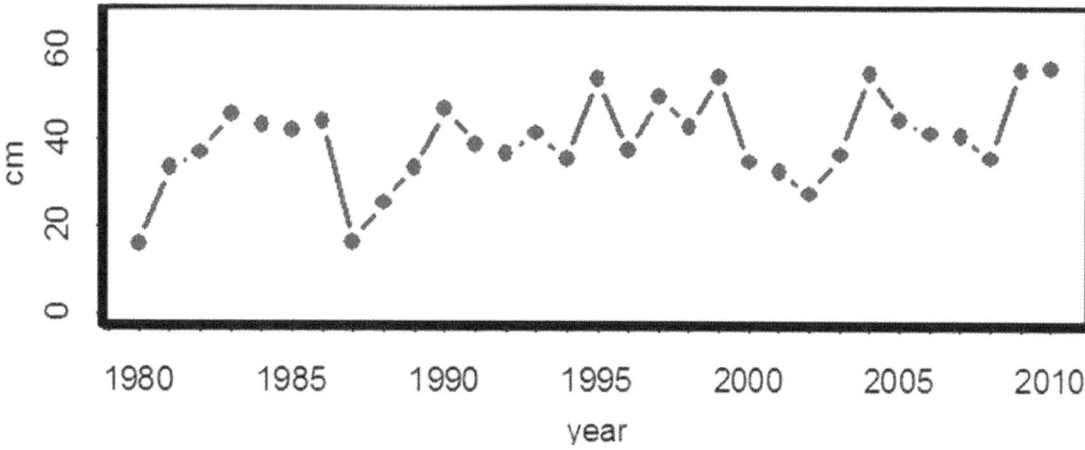

Figure 4b. Deposition, concentrations, and precipitation for Beaver Meadows.

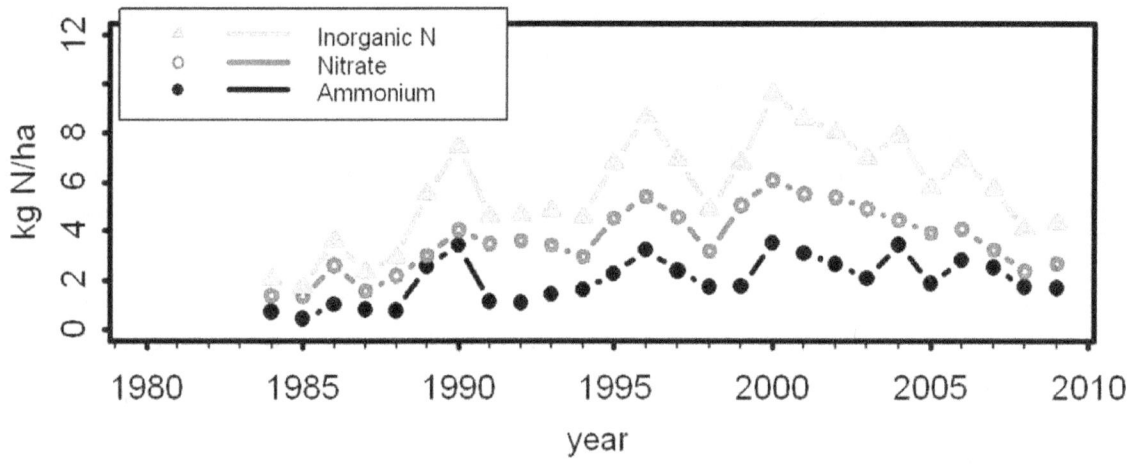

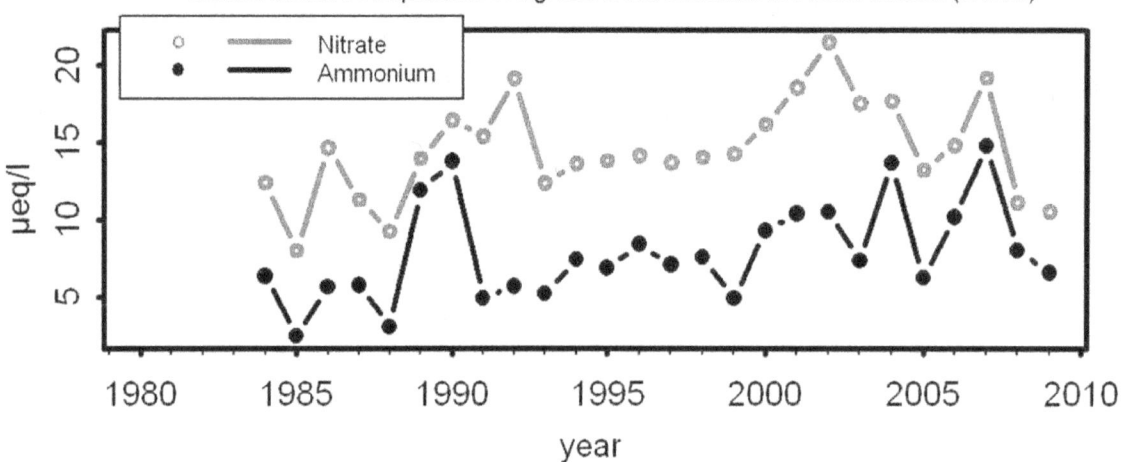

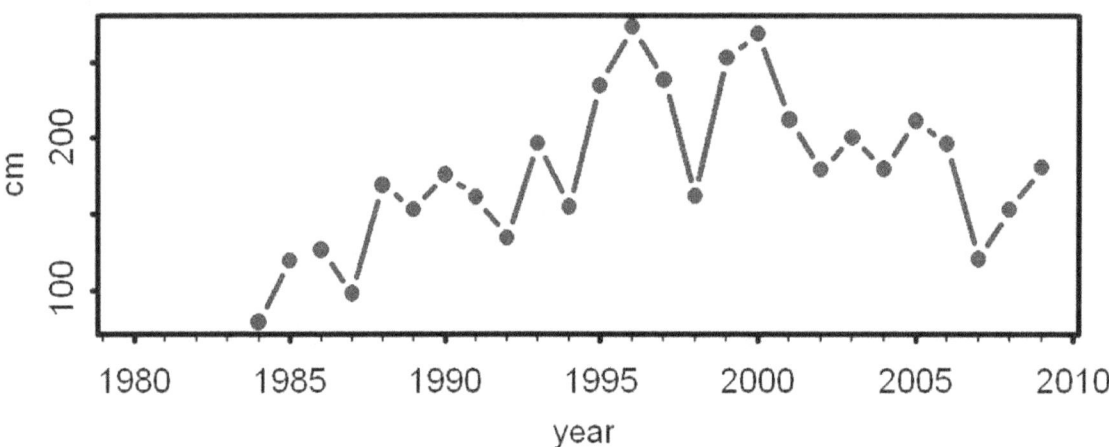

Figure 4c. Deposition, concentrations, and precipitation for Niwot Saddle.

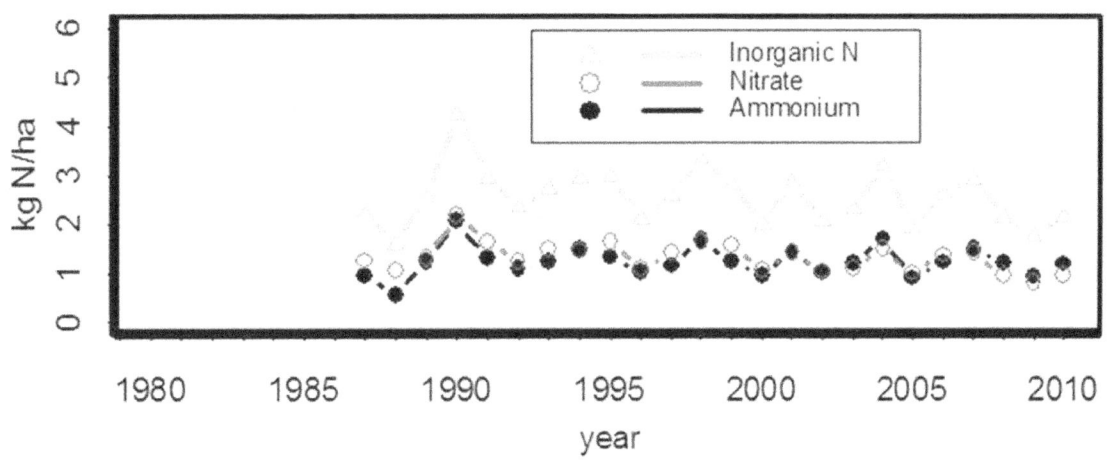

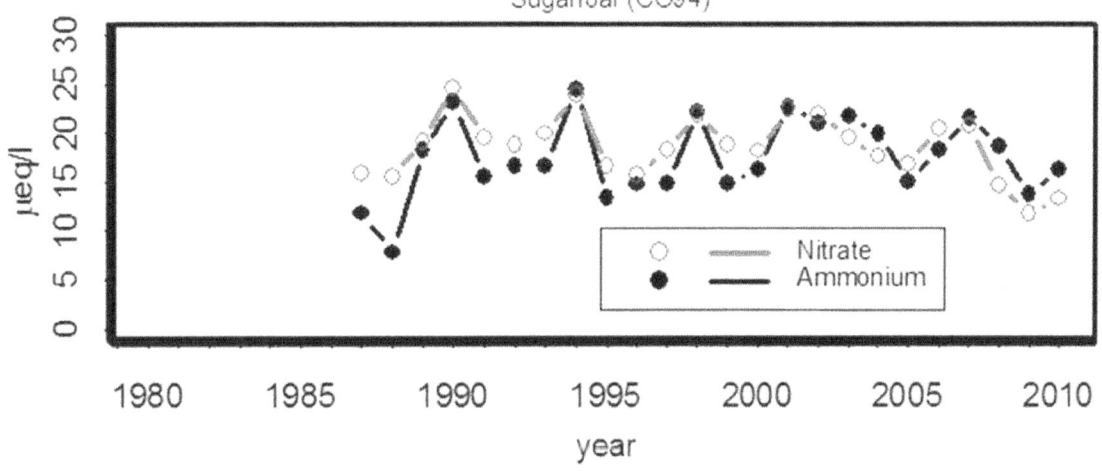

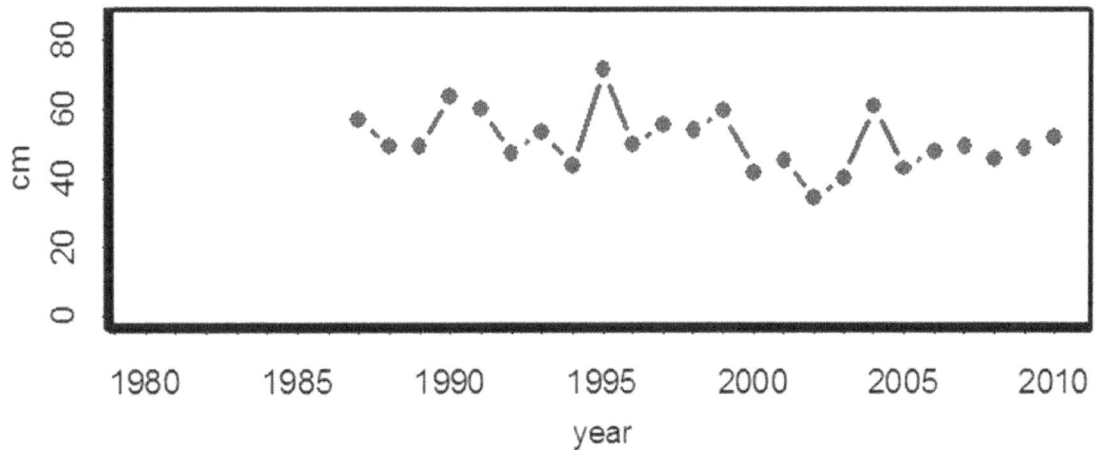

Figure 4d. Deposition, concentrations, and precipitation for Sugarloaf.

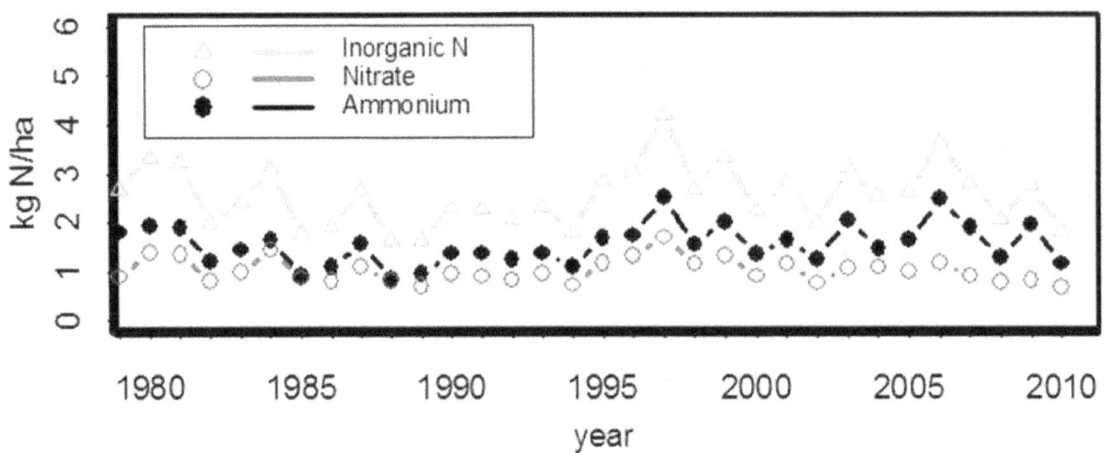

Annual Wet Deposition at Pawnee (CO22)

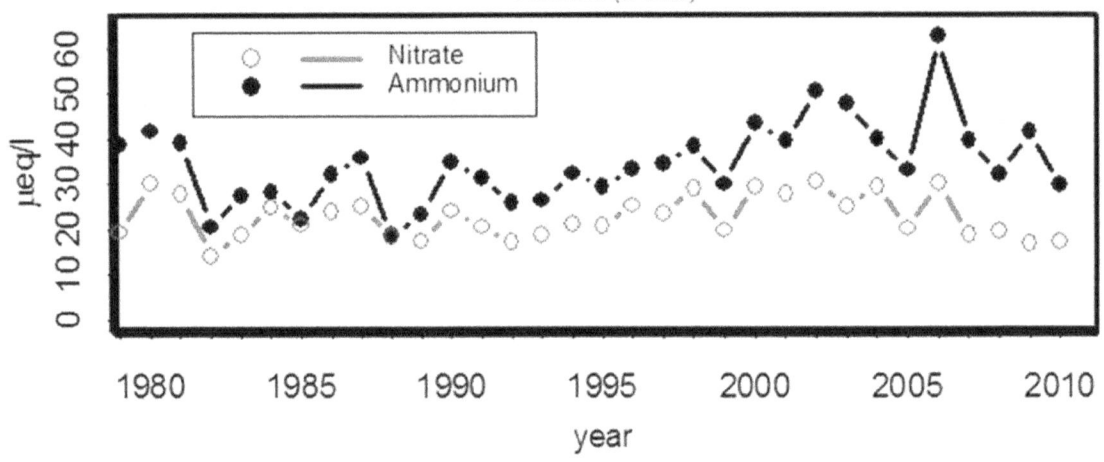

Mean Annual Precipitation Weighted Concentration at Pawnee (CO22)

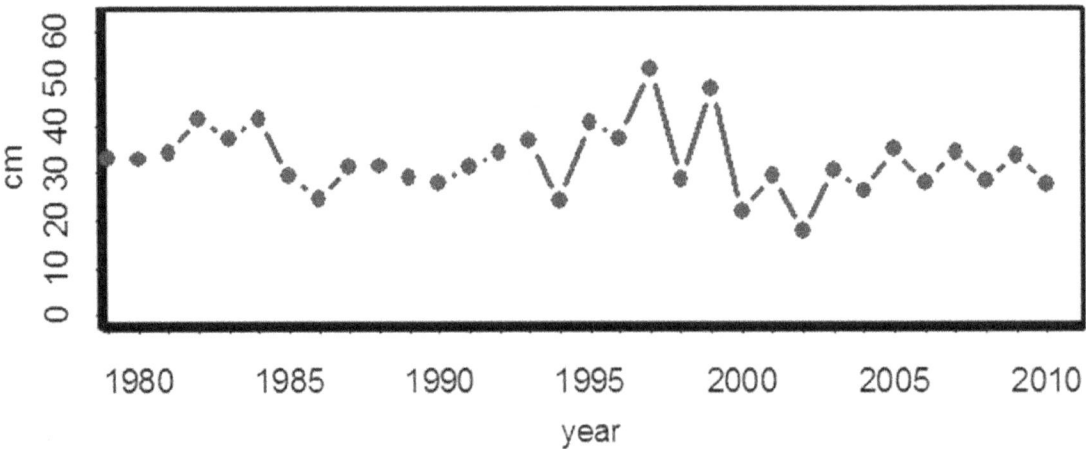

Annual Precipitation at Pawnee (CO22)

Figure 4e. Deposition, concentrations, and precipitation for Pawnee.

Table 2 shows results from the trend analysis for the entire period of record. Trends were evaluated for statistical significance at the 95% confidence level (p-value ≤ 0.05). Data were obtained from the NADP/NTN website and were screened according to the data completeness criteria in Appendix C. The data sets were reformatted and trends were computed using a computer code available through the USGS for the Kendall family of trend tests (Helsel and Frans 2006, http://pubs.usgs.gov/sir/2005/5275/pdf/sir2005-5275.pdf). Trends in deposition and precipitation were run on annual sum data using the Mann-Kendall test. Trends in precipitation-weighted mean concentrations were run on seasonal (quarterly) data using the Seasonal Kendall Test. The Seasonal Kendall Test was developed by the U.S. Geological Survey in the 1980s to analyze surface-water quality throughout the U.S. (Hirsch et al. 1982). The Seasonal Kendall Test is a non-parametric statistical test that is capable of detecting monotonic trends in data sets despite strong seasonality, missing data, and non-normal data distribution. The test has become one of the most frequently used to determine trends in environmental data (Helsel et al. 2006). Examples of the Seasonal Kendall Test used to determine trends in atmospheric deposition data include Lehmann et al. (2005, 2011) and Ingersoll et al. (2008). Appendix E contains a detailed description of the methods used for trends analysis in this report.

Statistically significant trends in wet nitrogen deposition were not detected at any of the NADP sites over the period of record. Previously, data from 2009 showed statically significant increases in wet nitrogen deposition for Beaver Meadows in RMNP (p-value = 0.031) and Niwot Saddle (p-value = 0.024) (National Park Service, 2011). With the addition of 2010 data, these trends in deposition are no

Table 2. Results from long-term trends over the period of record (through 2010)

Wet Nitrogen Deposition				
Site Name	Start Year	Trend (kg N/ha/yr)	P-value	Significant Trends
Loch Vale	1984	0.02	0.099	no trend
Beaver Meadows	1981	0.01	0.098	no trend
Niwot Saddle	1985	0.05	0.397	no trend
Sugarloaf	1987	-0.02	0.333	no trend
Pawnee	1980	0.01	0.551	no trend
Ammonium Precipitation-weighted Mean Concentrations				
Site Name	Start Year	Trend (µeq/L/yr)	P-value	Significant Trends
Loch Vale	1984	0.15	0.002	increasing
Beaver Meadows	1981	0.22	0.003	increasing
Niwot Saddle	1985	0.09	0.076	no trend
Sugarloaf	1987	0.14	0.140	no trend
Pawnee	1980	0.42	0.005	increasing
Nitrate Precipitation-weighted Mean Concentrations				
Site Name	Start Year	Trend (µeq/L/yr)	P-value	Significant Trends
Loch Vale	1984	0.03	0.591	no trend
Beaver Meadows	1981	-0.04	0.430	no trend
Niwot Saddle	1985	0.05	0.653	no trend
Sugarloaf	1987	-0.06	0.512	no trend
Pawnee	1980	-0.01	0.875	no trend
Precipitation				
Site Name	Start Year	Trend (cm/yr)	P-value	Significant Trends
Loch Vale	1984	-0.27	0.646	no trend
Beaver Meadows	1981	0.28	0.164	no trend
Niwot Saddle	1985	2.48	0.042	increasing
Sugarloaf	1987	-0.36	0.172	no trend
Pawnee	1980	-0.17	0.153	no trend

longer statistically significant. In contrast to deposition, precipitation-weighted ammonium concentrations increased significantly over the period of record at three of the five Front Range sites including Loch Vale, Beaver Meadows, and Pawnee (p-values < 0.005). There were no significant trends in precipitation-weighted nitrate concentrations at any sites over the period of record. A significant, increasing trend in precipitation amount was observed at Niwot Saddle (p-value = 0.042).

One goal of the NDRP is to "reverse the trend of increasing nitrogen deposition at the park." The analysis of long-term trends allows us to answer the question: Has nitrogen deposition decreased at RMNP and other sites in the region? A significant increasing trend in nitrogen deposition in the park was reported for 1984-2000 (p-value<0.05) (Burns 2003). Results from our analysis indicate that wet nitrogen deposition is not increasing or decreasing at RMNP or other sites in the region over the period of record. The only significant trends detected in the region were increasing ammonium concentrations at three of five sites and increasing precipitation at one site. Long-term trends at Loch Vale are similar to the other Front Range sites and show that data from Loch Vale are not anomalous. Therefore, nitrogen deposition is no longer increasing at RMNP for the 1984–2010 period, but is not decreasing either, at the park or other sites in the region over the period of record.

5.3. Short-term trends analyses for Rocky Mountain National Park and other regional sites

Changes in nitrogen concentrations and deposition over a more recent period of time are more relevant to recent changes in emissions. Trend analyses were run using the same parameters but over more recent time periods. Statistical trends are more difficult to detect using shorter-time periods so two time periods were evaluated covering the last 5 (2006–2010) and 7 (2004–2010) years. Table 3 shows the results of the trend analysis for the individual sites, identifying the statistically significant trends (p-value ≤ 0.05).

Wet nitrogen deposition at RMNP has not significantly decreased at Loch Vale or Beaver Meadows over the past 5 or 7 years. Precipitation-weighted ammonium concentrations significantly decreased at Beaver Meadows (p-value = 0.015) and Pawnee (p-value = 0.038) over the 7 year time period. Ammonium concentrations also significantly decreased at Pawnee over the 5 year time period (p-value = 0.017). Four sites showed significant decreases in precipitation-weighted nitrate concentrations in the 7 year time period (p-values 0.045) and three sites showed significant decreases in nitrate concentrations in the 5 year time frame (p-value < 0.035). Irrespective of significance, trend tendencies were all decreasing for nitrogen deposition, ammonium, and nitrate concentrations for both the 5 and 7 year time periods. There was a significant increase in precipitation amount at Loch Vale over the 5 year time period (p-value = 0.028).

The analysis of short-term trends allows us to answer the question: Has nitrogen deposition recently decreased at RMNP and at other sites in the region? Nitrogen deposition has not recently decreased at RMNP or other sites in the region. However, ammonium concentrations are decreasing at a few sites, and nitrate concentrations are decreasing at most sites in the region.

6. Summary

Achievement of the goals of the NDRP will be determined by the weight of evidence. The three analyses provided in this report indicate the following:

1. Wet nitrogen deposition in 2010 was above the glidepath.
2. Over the long term (1984–2010), wet nitrogen deposition has not decreased, but shows no trend at RMNP or other sites in the region.
3. In more recent years (2004–2010), wet nitrogen deposition has also not decreased, but shows no trend at RMNP or other sites in the region. Over the same period, however, nitrate concentrations have decreased significantly at most sites and ammonium concentrations have decreased significantly at a few sites in the region.

Table 3. Trend results for 5 year (2006–2010) and 7 year (2004–2010) time periods.

Wet Nitrogen Deposition

Site Name	5 year			7 year		
	Trend (kg N/ha/yr)	P-value	Significant Trends	Trend (kg N/ha/yr)	P-value	Significant Trends
Loch Vale	-0.12	0.221	no trend	-0.09	0.368	no trend
Beaver Meadows	-0.18	0.221	no trend	-0.20	0.071	no trend
Niwot Saddle	-0.58	0.462	no trend	-0.51	0.071	no trend
Sugarloaf	-0.24	0.462	no trend	-0.17	0.367	no trend
Pawnee	-0.39	0.086	no trend	-0.12	0.548	no trend

Ammonium Precipitation-weighted Mean Concentrations

Site Name	5 year			7 year		
	Trend (µeq/L/yr)	P-value	Significant Trends	Trend (µeq/L/yr)	P-value	Significant Trends
Loch Vale	-1.20	0.071	no trend	-0.35	0.525	no trend
Beaver Meadows	-5.90	0.059	no trend	-1.25	0.015	decreasing
Niwot Saddle	-1.73	0.089	no trend	-1.15	0.060	no trend
Sugarloaf	-2.32	0.270	no trend	-0.70	0.329	no trend
Pawnee	-5.97	0.017	decreasing	-2.99	0.038	decreasing

Nitrate Precipitation-weighted Mean Concentrations

Site Name	5 year			7 year		
	Trend (µeq/L/yr)	P-value	Significant Trends	Trend (µeq/L/yr)	P-value	Significant Trends
Loch Vale	-1.95	0.035	decreasing	-0.58	0.045	decreasing
Beaver Meadows	-2.12	0.090	no trend	-1.05	0.022	decreasing
Niwot Saddle	-1.76	0.003	decreasing	-1.45	0.007	decreasing
Sugarloaf	-2.60	0.005	decreasing	-0.70	0.329	no trend
Pawnee	-2.44	0.094	no trend	-2.99	0.038	decreasing

Precipitation

Site Name	5 year			7 year		
	Trend (cm/yr)	P-value	Significant Trends	Trend (cm/yr)	P-value	Significant Trends
Loch Vale	13.49	0.028	increasing	5.79	0.133	no trend
Beaver Meadows	4.25	0.462	no trend	0.18	1.000	no trend
Niwot Saddle	29.11	0.462	no trend	0.53	0.764	no trend
Sugarloaf	0.92	0.462	no trend	0.84	0.764	no trend
Pawnee	-0.20	0.806	no trend	-0.09	1.000	no trend

References

Baron, J. S. 2006. Hindcasting nitrogen deposition to determine an ecological critical load. *Ecological Applications* 16(2): 433–439.

Burns, D. A. 2003. Atmospheric nitrogen deposition in the Rocky Mountains of Colorado and Southern Wyoming, USA – a review and new analysis of past study results. *Environmental Pollution* 37:921–932.

Burns, D. A., J. A., Lynch, B. J., Cosby, M. E., Fenn, J. S., Baron, US EPA Clean Air Markets Division. 2011. National Acid Precipitation Assessment Program Report to Congress 2011: An Integrated Assessment. National Science and Technology Council, Washington, DC, 114 p. Available on the Internet at http://ny.water.usgs.gov/projects/NAPAP.

Clow, D. W., G. P. Ingersoll, M. A. Mast, J. T. Turk, D. H. Campbell. 2002. Comparison of snowpack and winter wet-deposition chemistry in the Rocky Mountains, USA: implications for winter dry deposition. *Atmospheric Environment* 36: 2337–2348.

Dentener, F. J. 2001. Personal communication with Tamara Blett, National Park Service. Globally modeled nitrogen maps for 1860.

Galloway, J. N., W. H. Schlesinger, H. Levy II, A. Michaels, J.L. Schnoor. 1995. Nitrogen fixation: Anthropogenic enhancement — environmental response. *Global Biogeochemical Cycles* 9(2): 235–252.

Galloway, J. N., W. C. Keene, G. E. Likens. 1996. Processes controlling the composition of precipitation at a remote Southern hemisphere location: Torres del Paine National Park, Chile. *Journal of Geophysical Research* 101(D3): 6883–6897.

Helsel, D. R. and L. M. Frans. 2006. Regional Kendall test for trend. *Environmental Science & Technology* 40(13): 4066–4073.

Helsel, D. R., D. K. Mueller, J. R. Slack. 2006. Computer program for the Kendall family of trend tests. U.S. Geological Survey Scientific Investigations Report 2005–5275, 4 pp. [http://pubs.usgs.gov/sir/2005/5275/pdf/sir2005-5275.pdf].

Hirsch, R. M., J. R. Slack, R. A. Smith. 1982. Techniques of trend analysis for monthly water quality data. *Water Resources Research* 18 107–121.

Ingersoll, G. P., M. A. Mast, D. H. Campbell, D. W. Clow, L. Nanus, J. T. Turk. 2008. Trends in snowpack chemistry and comparison to National Atmospheric Deposition Program results for the Rocky Mountains, U.S., 1993–2004. *Atmospheric Environment* 42: 6098–6113.

Ingersoll, G. P. 2010. Personal communication. U.S. Geologic Survey.

Lehmann, C. M. B., V. C. Bowersox, S. M. Larson. 2005. Spatial and temporal trends of precipitation chemistry in the United States, 1985–2002. *Environmental Pollution* 135: 347–361.

Lehmann, C. M. B., D. A. Gay. 2011. Monitoring long-term trends of acidic wet deposition in US precipitation: results from the National Atmospheric Deposition Program. *Power Plant Chemistry* 13(7): 386–393.

National Park Service, Air Resources Division. 2011. 2009 monitoring and tracking wet nitrogen deposition at Rocky Mountain National Park: September 2011, Natural Resource Report NPS/NRSS/ARD/NRR-2011/442. National Park Service, Denver, Colorado.

Richer, E. E. J. S. Baron. 2011. Loch Vale Watershed long-term ecological research and monitoring program: Quality assurance report, 2003–09. U.S. Geological Survey Open-File Report 2011–1137, 22 p.

U. S. Environmental Protection Agency (U.S. EPA). 2011. 2010 Progress Report: Emission, compliance, and market analyses. Washington, DC: U.S. EPA. August. Available on the Internet at http://www.epa.gov/airmarkets/progress/ARPCAIR10_01.html.

U. S. Environmental Protection Agency (U.S. EPA). 2012. 2010 Progress Report: Environmental and health results. Washington, DC: U.S. EPA. June. Available on the Internet at http://www.epa.gov/airmarkets/progress/ARPCAIR10.html.

U. S. Environmental Protection Agency (U.S. EPA). 2010. United States – Canada Air Quality Agreement Progress Report 2012. EPA-430-R-10-011. Washington, DC: U.S. EPA. October. Available on the Internet at http://www.epa.gov/airmarkets/progsregs/usca/docs/2010report.pdf.

U.S. Geological Survey. 2011. Evaluation of National Atmospheric Deposition Program measurements for co-located sites CO89 and CO98 at Rocky Mountain National Park, 2010. U.S. Geological Survey Cooperator Report, 21 p.

Wetherbee, G. A., N.E. Latysh, J. D. Gordon. 2005. Spatial and temporal variability of the overall error of National Atmospheric Deposition Program measurements determined by the USGS collocated-sampler program, water years 1989–2001. *Environmental Pollution* 135: 407–418.

Williams, M.W., T. Bardsley, M. Rikkers. 1998. Overestimation of snow depth and inorganic nitrogen wetfall using NADP data, Niwot Ridge, Colorado. *Atmospheric Environment* 32: 3827–3833.

Appendix A: A History of the Loch Vale NAPD/NTN Monitoring Site

The Loch Vale NADP/NTN site was established in the summer of 1983, when the original Aerochem Metrics Model 301 precipitation collector and mechanical Belfort rain gage were installed (NADP/NTN site CO98). In 2006, after extensive laboratory and field testing, the NADP/NTN approved two new electronic rain gages, including the ETI NOAH IV. During the summer of 2007, a NOAH IV rain gage was installed at the Loch Vale site. The original Belfort and the new NOAH IV operated side-by-side for two years (2008 and 2009). Differences in recorded precipitation (approximately 5 percent) were negligible (National Park Service, 2011: Richer and Baron, 2011). A second and temporary co-located NADP/NTN site (CO89) was installed at Loch Vale in the fall of 2009 for quality assurance assessments. The current site consists of two precipitation collectors and two NOAH IV rain gages on satellite telemetry. The original Belfort rain gage was removed during the summer of 2010 in an effort to keep the monitoring site footprint to a minimum in accordance with the park's Wilderness Designation. In summer of 2011, two ammonia passive samplers were installed in the park as part of the NADP Ammonia Monitoring Network (AMoN); one at the Loch Vale NADP monitoring site (NADP/AMoN site CO98) and one near the Long's Peak Ranger Station at the Clean Air Status and Trends Network (CASTNet) site (NADP/AMoN site CO88). In fall 2011, the four solar panels were replaced with two more efficient, less reflective panels and moved to a location of less snow accumulation.

Loch Vale NADP/NTN monitoring site history.	
Date	**Event**
Summer 1983	Site installed with precipitation collector and original Belfort rain gage (NADP/NTN site CO98).
Summer 2007	NOAH IV rain gage added (intended to replace Belfort rain gage, once differences were documented).
Fall 2009	Co-located site (NADP/NTN site CO89) and telemetry installed, solar power and storage increased.
Summer 2010	Belfort rain gage removed.
Summer 2011	Passive ammonia samplers installed NADP/AMoN (site CO98 and site CO88)
Fall 2011	Solar panels replaced and relocated.

Appendix B: Explanation of NADP/NTN Terms and Calculations

The NADP/NTN collects weekly precipitation samples and records precipitation amount. Concentrations of sulfate, nitrate, chloride, ammonium, and base cations are determined by laboratory analysis and reported in units of mg/L. Hydrogen ion is reported as pH. Weekly precipitation samples are aggregated into precipitation-weighted mean concentrations for monthly, seasonal, and annual time periods by using Equation (1).

$$\overline{C}_{ppt\ wt} = \frac{\sum_{i=1}^{n}\left(C_{w,i} \times P_{w,i}\right)}{\sum_{i=1}^{n} P_{w,i}} \qquad \text{(Eq. 1)}$$

where:

$\overline{C}_{ppt\ wt}$ = precipitation-weighted mean concentration, mg/L

$C_{w,i}$ = precipitation concentration for individual event, mg/L

$P_{w,i}$ = Precipitation depth for individual event, cm

n = number of events

Precipitation-weighted mean concentrations are used in order to simulate having one composite sample over the time period of interest. For example, a precipitation-weighted mean concentration for one year (or month or season) is equivalent to adding all of the weekly samples together into one sample and then determining the concentration of ions in that sample.

Example: sample concentration and precipitation amount.

Sample	Concentration	Precipitation Amount
1	15 mg/L	1 cm
2	5 mg/L	6 cm

A precipitation-weighted mean concentration is more representative of the average concentration of the majority of the precipitation. In the above example, the precipitate on-weighted mean concentration is 6.43 mg/L[(15 x 1 + 5x6)/(1+6)] and is more heavily influenced by the larger precipitation event, whereas an arithmetic mean is 10 mg/L.

Precipitation concentrations can also be presented in terms of microequivalents per liter (μeq/L). An equivalent is defined as a mass of an element that can combine with 1 gram of hydrogen in a chemical reaction. It is a way of normalizing for ionic charge. Nitrate ion has one negative charge (NO_3^-) and ammonium has one positive charge (NH_4^+), once converted to μeq/L the ion concentrations can be compared to each other. Concentrations in mg/L are converted to μeq/L by using the factors listed in following table.

Conversion factors for ion concentrations, mg/L to µeq/L.	
Ion	**Conversion Factor**
Ammonium	1 mg/L = 55.4371 µeq/L
Nitrate	1 mg/L = 16.12776 µeq/L

Wet deposition is calculated by multiplying the precipitation-weighted mean concentration for a period of time by the total amount of precipitation during that time (Equation 2).

$$D_w = \overline{C}_{ppt\ wt} \times P_{TOT} \times 10^{-1} \qquad \text{(Eq. 2)}$$

where:

D_w = wet deposition, kg/ha

$\overline{C}_{ppt\ wt}$ = precipitation-weighted mean concentration, mg/L

P_{TOT} = total precipitation depth for period, cm

Nitrogen deposition is calculated by summing the nitrogen (N) from nitrate (NO_3) deposition and ammonium (NH_4) deposition as shown in (Equation 3). The conversion factors in the equation represent the molecular weight ratios of N to NH_4 and NO_3, respectively.

$$D_{IN} = \left(D_{NH_4^+} \times \frac{14.01}{18.01} \right) + \left(D_{NO_3^-} \times \frac{14.01}{62.01} \right) \qquad \text{(Eq. 3)}$$

where:

D_{IN} = wet deposition of N, kg/ha

$D_{NH_4^+}$ = wet deposition of NH_4, kg/ha

$D_{NO_3^-}$ = wet deposition of NO_3, kg/ha

Appendix C: Data Completeness Criteria

Quality assurance is stressed in all aspects of NADP operations. Sites are required to meet minimum siting standards, use approved instruments, and follow standard procedures. The NADP analytical laboratory operates under well-defined quality assurance programs with well-defined quality control criteria. Quality assurance (QA) continues for processing, coding, and reporting data to the web. NADP QA programs provide representative data of documented completeness to assist data users in evaluating the appropriateness of the data for the intended application. NADP provides data users with several data completeness criteria including:

Criterion 1 – Percentage of time during the year for which valid samples are available.

Criterion 2 – Percentage of time during the year for which valid precipitation amounts are available.

Criterion 3 – Percentage of the total measured precipitation associated with valid samples for the year.

Criterion 4 – Percentage of the total precipitation measured by the rain gage that is represented by the collected sample volume. Criterion 4 was eliminated in 2008 per the recommendations of the NADP Quality Assurance Advisory Group (http://nadp.isws.illinois.edu/lib/misc/Criterion4report.pdf).

The NADP uses data completeness criteria values ≥ 75 for criteria 1 and 3, and ≥ 90 for criterion 2 in order to screen data for the annual isopleth map summaries. However, data users may select different values, depending upon the intended application of the data. For example, Lehmann et al. (2005) determined that data completeness criteria values ≥ 50 for criteria 1 and 3, and ≥ 75 for criterion 2 were sufficient for long-term trends analyses. Data presented in this report will include all seasons and years with Criterion 2 ≥ 90 percent, regardless of other criteria completeness, based on the following rationale. Using this criterion, 3% of the data were excluded from this report including one year of data for Beaver Meadows (1987) and 3 years of data for Niwot Saddle (1985, 1990, and 1991). No seasons were excluded for any sites.

Criterion 1. This measure indicates how much of the year is represented by samples. Although it is important to collect precipitation samples throughout the year, it is less important at high elevation sites where precipitation inputs are highly seasonal. For example, at a site like Loch Vale, there could be valid samples representing 80% of the year; however, if samples for the months of March and April were invalid, a significant portion of the wet deposition would have been missed. Therefore, Criterion 1 is not critical to the purposes of this study, and was not used to screen data in this report.

Criterion 2. This measure indicates how much of the year is represented by rain gage data. It is extremely important to be able to accurately measure precipitation amount in order to accurately estimate wet deposition at a site. In order to be used in this report, 90% of the year will need to have valid precipitation measurements. Therefore, seasons and years of data with Criterion 2 ≥ 90 percent are included in this report.

Criterion 3. This measure indicates how much of the measured precipitation is associated with valid samples. In the spring and summer, samples are occasionally invalidated due to visible contamination (i.e. plant material, dust, bird droppings, insects, etc.) that occurs in combination with anomalous sample chemistry relative to historical sample chemistry. However, the majority of invalidated samples occur during the fall and winter due to equipment problems or inadequate solar power supply. For example, samples are considered invalid when the lid of the collector has remained open for 6 hours or more after the last record of precipitation, resulting in dry exposure of the sample. However, comparison of winter wetfall chemistry as measured by NADP with co-located snowpack samples indicates annual and seasonal concentrations computed by NADP are representative of winter precipitation chemistry, even excluding invalidated winter samples. Snowpack chemistry has been monitored by the USGS in the Rocky Mountains since 1993 including 14 co-located sites (http://co.water.usgs.gov/projects/RM_snowpack/index.html). Full depth snowpack samples are collected at the time of maximum snowpack accumulation (approximately in April) and represent deposition for the entire winter period. Clow et al. 2002 showed that the chemistry of winter-time NADP samples and snowpack samples (from 1992–1999) are not significantly different for nitrate concentrations (p-value = 0.2537). Snowpack samples had slightly higher concentrations of ammonium (p-value < 0.0001), and it was suggested that NADP may underestimate ammonium. This analysis has recently been updated with data from 2000–2011 and shows similar results. Nitrate concentrations were not significantly different (p-value = 0.206) and ammonium concentrations were slightly higher in snowfall (p-value = 0.0002). This shows that winter-time samples that are invalid due to dry exposure have little effect on the representativeness of the winter chemistry data. Because most precipitation at this site is in the form of snow, the data record at Loch Vale is considered sufficient to characterize deposition at the site and Criterion 3 will not be used to exclude data from this report.

Furthermore, data from the co-located site at Loch Vale allows us to compare the data record for Loch Vale (CO98) to a combined data record where data from the co-located site (CO89) are used to fill in when there are invalid values for Loch Vale. In 2010, there were 17 invalid samples for Loch Vale, the majority of which occurred in the winter. The table below shows that with the more complete record, the mean annual ammonium concentration declined from 0.13 to 0.12 and the mean annual nitrate concentration declined from 0.54 to 0.52 mg/L. Annual nitrogen deposition decreased from 2.98 to 2.83 kg /ha/yr, a 5% difference. Ideally, valid samples are desired for every week of the year. However, these samples are collected in harsh, remote locations, and the loss of power and equipment malfunctions sometimes result in invalidated samples. This analysis shows that the effect of invalid samples on annual values is small. Efforts will continue to maximize the collection of valid samples (see Section 4 for details).

Comparison of Loch Vale (CO98) data to augmented data in 2010.						
2010	**CO98 Data**			**CO98 Data Augmented with CO89 Records for Invalid Data**		
	NH_4	NO_3	N	NH_4	NO_3	N
Precipitation-weighted Mean Concentration (mg/L)	0.13	0.54		0.12	0.52	
Wet Deposition (kg N/ha)	1.38	1.60	2.98	1.27	1.56	2.83

Appendix D: Evaluation of National Atmospheric Deposition Program Measurements for Co-located Sites CO89 and CO98 at Rocky Mountain National Park, 2010

By Greg Wetherbee, U.S. Geological Survey

National Atmospheric Deposition Program/National Trends Network (NADP/NTN) sites CO89 and CO98 are located at approximately 3,159 meters (m) altitude; 40.2878 degrees north latitude;105.6628 degrees west longitude, in Rocky Mountain National Park, Colorado. Each site has a precipitation gage for depth measurement and a precipitation collector for sample collection for chemical analysis. The collectors are spaced approximately 6.2 m apart, and the rain gages are spaced approximately 6.5 m apart horizontally and 0.5 m vertically. The CO89 site was installed in 2009 to collect data for comparison to the CO98 data. This report presents an estimation of error based on measured differences in data collected at co-located NADP sites CO89 and CO98. The results presented herein are for calendar year 2010, the first full calendar year of co-located site data collection at CO89.

A comparison of precipitation depths, sample volumes, concentration, and deposition differences at the two sites is presented. Daily precipitation depths were obtained from the NADP web site: http://nadp.isws.illinois.edu/precip/. Chemical analysis results and sample volumes for weekly wet-deposition samples were obtained from the NADP web site: http://nadp.isws.illinois.edu/data/. Field and laboratory processes were identical for the two sites. All samples were analyzed by the NADP Central Analytical Laboratory in Champaign, Illinois. Sample collection methods are available at: http://nadp.isws.uiuc.edu/lib/manuals/opman.pdf. Sample analysis methods are available on the CAL web site at: http://nadpweb.sws.uiuc.edu/ops/cal/SOPs%20Final/Forms/SOPs.aspx.

All weekly paired samples with sufficient volume for analysis without dilution that were not flagged by NADP as contaminated were used to evaluate the overall

Annual precipitation-weighted mean concentrations and total deposition values for National Atmospheric Deposition Program / National Trends Network sites CO89 and CO98 during 2010.

Analyte (units)	Annual precipitation-weighted mean concentration (units)		Annual precipitation-weighted mean concentration differences* (percent)	Annual total deposition (kg/ha)		Annual total deposition differences* (percent)
	CO89	CO98		CO89	CO98	
Calcium (mg/L)	0.467	0.280	-40.2	6.33	3.69	-41.7
Magnesium (mg/L)	0.029	0.020	-31.0	.39	0.26	-32.7
Potassium (mg/L)	0.024	0.019	-19.8	.32	0.25	-21.8
Sodium (mg/L)	0.029	0.025	-15.5	.40	0.33	-17.6
Ammonium (mg/L as NH₄⁺)	0.120	0.135	11.9	1.63	1.78	9.2
Nitrate (mg/L as NO3-)	0.498	0.537	7.9	6.73	7.09	5.2
Total Nitrogen (mg/L as N)	0.206	0.226	9.7	2.79	2.98	7.0
Chloride (mg/L)	0.038	0.041	9.7	0.51	0.54	6.9
Sulfate (mg/L as SO₄²⁻)	0.309	0.303	-1.9	4.18	4.00	-4.3
Hydrogen Ion (µeq/L from pH)	4.709	4.856	3.1	.06	.06	0.6

* Differences calculated as CO98-minus-CO89 divided by CO89. [mg/L, milligrams per liter; kg/ha, killograms per hectare; µeq/L, microequivalents per liter]

measurement error based on differences in solute concentration, specific conductance, and sample volume. Paired relative differences were obtained by subtracting the CO89 site values from the CO98 site values. Complete chemical analyses were available for 44 valid samples from CO89 and 35 valid samples from CO98. Substitution of 11 days of missing CO98 precipitation-depth record with values from CO89, which is a standard NADP practice, was done to evaluate differences in total annual deposition values.

A brief summary of the results is provided here, however, the full report is available at http://nature.nps.gov /air/pubs/pdf/USGS_2011Co-located_sites-at-RMNP.pdf.

Median absolute percent differences in weekly ammonium, nitrate, and sulfate concentrations were 8.6, 7.5, and 9.7 percent, respectively. Weekly concentration differences between the two sites were statistically significant (α=0.1) for nitrate, chloride, and sulfate. Weekly sample volume differences were also statistically significant whereby CO98 collected more volume for 59 percent of the samples.

Annual precipitation-weighted mean concentration values are shown in the table and were higher for CO98 compared to CO89 for ammonium (11.9 percent), nitrate (7.9 percent), and total nitrogen (9.7 percent), but lower for sulfate (-1.9 percent). Annual total deposition values were higher for CO98 compared to CO89 for ammonium (9.2 percent), nitrate (5.2 percent), and total nitrogen (7.0 percent), but lower for sulfate (-4.3 percent).

This analysis and future comparisons will allow us to evaluate uncertainty in the data. However, the data from the original NADP site at Loch Vale (CO98) will always be used to compare to the glidepath because the resource management goal is based on hindcasting of data from this site.

Reference

U.S. Geological Survey. 2011. Evaluation of National Atmospheric Deposition Program Measurements for Co-located Sites CO89 and CO98 at Rocky Mountain National Park, 2010. U.S. Geological Survey Cooperator Report, 21 p.

Appendix E: Methods of testing trends in NADP precipitation chemistry data utilized by the Rocky Mountain National Park Deposition Tracking Project

By M. Alisa Mast, U.S. Geological Survey

The Rocky Mountain National Park Deposition Tracking Project will run trends in precipitation chemistry once a year for the parameters and sites listed below using the trend methods described in this document. The Seasonal Kendall Test (SKT) was used to evaluate trends in ammonium and nitrate concentrations in precipitation, which is consistent with other publications on trends in precipitation chemistry (Lehmann 2005 and 2011). The SKT performs a Mann-Kendall Test (MKT) for individual seasons of the year then combines the results into one overall test. Using the SKT increases the power of the trend test by increasing the n to four seasons. However, the MKT was used for trends in nitrogen deposition and precipitation amount, because the SKT and MKT produce identical results for data sets with one season (e.g. annual data). Using the SKT for deposition and precipitation gives seasonal trend slopes that are 4 times too low.

The SKT and MKT tests can be run using a computer code available from the USGS (Helsel and others, 2006). The computer code (Kendall.exe) and example files can be downloaded at http://pubs.usgs.gov/sir/2005 /5275/downloads/.

A report describing the trend program is available at http://pubs.usgs.gov/sir/2005/5275/pdf/sir2005-5275.pdf.

NADP sites

- CO98 - Loch Vale
- CO19 - Beaver Meadows
- CO02 - Niwot Saddle
- CO94 - Sugarloaf
- CO22 - Pawnee

Parameters

- Seasonal Precipitation-weighted mean NH_4 concentrations in µeq/L/yr (winter, spring, summer, fall)
- Seasonal Precipitation-weighted mean NO_3 concentrations in µeq/L/yr (winter, spring, summer, fall)
- Annual Inorganic Nitrogen deposition in kg N/ha/yr
- Annual precipitation amount in cm

Time frame

- Period of Record (POR)
- 5 year
- 7 year

Trend Tests

- Seasonal Kendall Test (SKT) for seasonal concentrations (NH_4 and NO_3)
- Mann Kendall Test (MKT) for annual Inorganic Nitrogen deposition and precipitation amount

Procedure

1. Retrieve Data

Annual and seasonal precipitation chemistry data can be retrieved from the National Atmospheric Deposition Program (NADP) web site at http://nadp.isws.illinois.edu/NTN/ntnData.aspx. Use "Custom Site List" to create a list and pull data for the 5 stations of interest (CO98, CO19, CO02, CO94, and CO22).

Retrieve seasonal data (winter, spring, summer, fall) for precipitation-weighted mean concentrations (in µeq/L) and annual data for deposition (in kg/ha/yr) and precipitation amount (in cm). Retrieve annual data based on calendar years (January to December). The seasonal and annual averages are computed by NADP using only valid samples. The winter seasonal data include the months of December, January, and February. Spring includes March, April, and May. Summer includes June, July, and August. Fall includes September, October, and November.

Pull data for the entire period of record in tab or comma delimited format and import into Excel or Access for further file formatting. In order to run the program you must remove all -9s from the file and replace with empty cells. Remove the first year of data from each station if it is incomplete (most stations began operation in the summer or fall months so the first year represents a partial year of data). Screen data using the NADP completeness criteria described in Appendix C.

2. Trend Calculations

This section describes how to set up input files and run the Seasonal Kendall test (SKT) and Mann-Kendall test (MKT) using the NADP data. Annual data (one season per year) tested with the SKT yields the same result as a Mann-Kendall test. Therefore, both seasonal and annual results can be tested using the method outlined below.

The first line of each input file should follow this format:

    2 0   NH4 Concentrations Station CO02

It is important to have "2" in column 1 of line 1 and "0" in column 3 of line 1. A description can be added starting in column 9. The next lines of the file contain the data with Year in the first column, Season (winter = 1, spring = 2, summer = 3, fall = 4) in the second column and the Value (e.g. concentration) in the third column. The final files will be space delimited and should look something like the examples below. For annual deposition and precipitation data, set the season equal to 1 for all years. Delete any lines with missing values.

Example input file for seasonal data:

```
2 0       NH4 Concentrations Station CO02
2006 1 3.71
2006 2 7.37
2006 3 16.85
2006 4 17.02
2007 1 4.21
2007 2 19.84
2007 3 26.22
2007 4 9.48
2008 1 5.76
2008 2 13.80
2008 3 14.85
2008 4 6.59
2009 1 3.27
2009 2 10.25
2009 3 8.87
2009 4 6.59
2010 1 5.32
2010 2 8.09
2010 3 9.53
2010 4 8.56
```

Example input file for annual data:

```
2 0       Inorganic Nitrogen Station CO22
2006 1 3.86    Note: set season equal to 1 for all years
2007 1 2.70
2008 1 2.12
2009 1 2.71
2010 1 1.66
```

To compute a trend, copy the "Kendall.exe" file into the directory that contains the input file. Double click on the Kendall.exe icon to start the program. Enter the input file name (e.g. NH4CO22.txt) and provide a name for the output file to which the results are written (e.g.NH4CO22out.txt).

An example of the output file is shown below. In this example, the trend was 0.3930 μeq/L/yr with a p-value of 0.0089. Because the period of record was longer than 10 years the adjusted p-value should be reported. This adjustment corrects for serial correlation in the dataset.

Example output file:

Seasonal Kendall Test for Trend

US Geological Survey, 2005

Data set: NH4 Station CO22

The record is 31 complete calendar years with 4 seasons per year beginning in year 1980.

The tau correlation coefficient is 0.219

$S = 407.$

$z = 3.450$

$p = 0.0006$

$p = 0.0089$ adjusted for correlation among seasons (such as serial dependence)

The adjusted p-value should be used only for data with more than 10 annual values per season.

The estimated trend may be described by the equation:

$Y = 22.48 + 0.3930 * \text{Time}$

where Time = Year (as a decimal) - 1979.75 (beginning of first water year)

References

Helsel, D. R., D. K. Mueller, J. R. Slack. 2006. Computer program for the Kendall family of trend tests. U.S. Geological Survey Scientific Investigations Report 2005–5275, 4 pp. Available at http://pubs.usgs.gov/sir/2005/5275/pdf/sir2005-5275.pdf.

Lehmann, C. M. B., V. C. Bowersox, S. M. Larson. 2005. Spatial and temporal trends of precipitation chemistry in the United States, 1985–2002. *Environmental Pollution* 135: 347–361.

Lehmann, C. M. B., D. A. Gay. 2011. Monitoring long-term trends of acidic wet deposition in US precipitation: results from the National Atmospheric Deposition Program. *Power Plant Chemistry* 13(7): 386–393.

NPS 121/116432, August 2012